NOVA SCOTIA TRAVEL GUIDE 2023-2024

A Complete Guide To Exploring Canada's Maritime History And The Bluenose Island

JAMES L. LOPEZ

Copyright © 2023 James L. Lopez

All rights reserved. No part of this book may be reproduced, stored in a retrieval system, or transmitted in any form or by any means, electronic, mechanical, photocopying, recording, or otherwise, without the prior written permission of the publisher, except in the case of brief quotations embodied in critical articles and reviews.

Table of contents

INTRODUCTION 6

    Brief History 9

    Climate and Weather.. 13

    Culture.. 16

CHAPTER 1: PLANNING YOUR TRIP 21

    When Is the Best Time to Visit? 21

    Visas & Entry Requirements 22

    Budgeting... 25

    Packing Tips for a Fantastic Vacation 28

        1. Weather-Responsive Clothing 28

        2. Comfortable Footwear 28

        3. Outdoor Requirements 28

        4. Swimsuits... 29

        5. Travel Documents and Needs 29

CHAPTER 2: EXPLORING THE BEAUTY OF NOVA SCOTIA 31

A Journey through Its Historical Places 31

Museums & Art Galleries: Cultural Heritage 34

CHAPTER 3: FOOD AND DINING 39

Exploring Local Cuisine and Specialties 39

Top Restaurants and Cafés for Culinary Delights 41

CHAPTER 4: NIGHTLIFE AND ENTERTAINMENT
.... 47

Exploring Activities and Entertainment 47

   1. Coastal Excursions 47

   2. Waterfront Treats 48

   3. Cultural Inclusion 48

   4. Festivals and Special Events 48

   5. Culinary Delights 49

   6. Entertainment and Art 49

   7. Beach Vacations 49

   9. Nightlife and Music 50

A Haven for Outdoor Enthusiasts 51

   Hiking Adventures: Discovering Nature's Glory .. 51

Kayaking & Canoeing in Paradise 52

Whale Watching: Marvel at Majestic Giants 53

Festivals, Museums, and Historic Sites 54

Discovering Regional Cuisine and Seafood Delights 57

Culinary Delights: Edible Gifts 61

Exploring Charming Nova Scotia's Bars and Pubs ... 65

Performances and live music 69

CHAPTER 5: ACCOMMODATION AND TRANSPORTATION 73

Hotels and Resorts Exquisite Getaways 73

Bed & Breakfast 76

Campgrounds and RV Parks 79

How to Get Around 82

The Top 5 Hotels in Nova Scotia for Luxurious Retreats 85

Safety Recommendations 88

Emergency Phone Numbers 91

Health and Medical Services 94

Basic Phrases 97

BONUS: CURATED SEASONAL EVENT CALENDAR.. 101

NOVA SCOTIA TRAVEL JOURNAL

INTRODUCTION

Welcome to a journey that will take you on a captivating adventure through the heart of Canada's Maritime Beauty – Nova Scotia. Within these pages, you will discover a land of boundless wonder, where rugged coastlines, charming fishing villages, and rich cultural heritage converge to create an experience unlike any other.

Nova Scotia, the "New Scotland," aptly embraces its name, a testament to its deep-rooted Celtic heritage, which resonates throughout the province's landscapes and traditions. As you delve into this travel guide, you will find yourself immersed in a tapestry of stories, both old and new, of a land that has withstood the test of time.

But Nova Scotia is much more than a history lesson. It is a living, breathing, and evolving destination that invites you to explore its untamed wilderness, serene lakes, and rolling hills. From the dramatic cliffs of the Cabot Trail to the idyllic shores of the South Shore, each corner of Nova Scotia boasts its own unique charm and allure.

Yet, beyond its stunning scenery, what truly sets Nova Scotia apart is the warmth and hospitality of its people. As you journey through this enchanting province, you will encounter a tapestry of communities, each with its distinct personality and traditions. From the bustling streets of Halifax to the intimate gatherings in small fishing towns, you will be welcomed with open arms and genuine smiles.

In this guide, we aim to unlock the secrets of Nova Scotia, to guide you to hidden gems and iconic landmarks alike. Whether you are a seasoned explorer or a first-time visitor, our curated itineraries, insider tips, and heartfelt recommendations will enable you to create lasting memories and forge connections with the essence of Nova Scotia.

Embrace the culinary delights that showcase the bounty of the sea and the richness of the land. Partake in vibrant festivals that celebrate the province's cultural mosaic and artistic flair. Engage in outdoor activities that beckon the adventurer in you, from hiking and kayaking to whale watching and star gazing.

As you turn each page, we hope you will feel the passion and affection we hold for Nova Scotia. This guide is a tribute to the province's magnificence and a testament to the life-changing experiences it offers to those willing to explore its wonders.

So, let the journey begin. Pack your curiosity, leave your worries behind, and set forth on an expedition to discover the heart and soul of Nova Scotia. The wonders that await you are beyond imagination, and the memories you will create are bound to be treasured forever.

Brief History

Nova Scotia, a picturesque province situated on the eastern coast of Canada, boasts a rich and diverse history that spans thousands of years. From its early Indigenous inhabitants to the arrival of European explorers and settlers, Nova Scotia has witnessed significant events that have shaped its culture, economy, and society. Let's embark on a journey through time to explore the fascinating history of Nova Scotia.

Indigenous Origins:

Before European contact, the region now known as Nova Scotia was inhabited by various Indigenous peoples, including the Mi'kmaq, Maliseet, Passamaquoddy, and Abenaki. These tribes lived in harmony with the land, relying on hunting, fishing, and agriculture for sustenance. Their profound connection with nature is evident in their spiritual beliefs and intricate artistry, exemplified by petroglyphs and pictographs found throughout the province.

European Exploration and Colonization

The early 16th century saw the arrival of European explorers on Nova Scotia's shores. John Cabot, a Venetian explorer, is believed to have been among the first to explore the region in 1497. However, it was French explorer Samuel de Champlain who played a pivotal role in establishing lasting European presence. In 1605, he founded Port Royal (now Annapolis Royal), which marked the beginning of French colonization in the area.

Struggle for Dominance

Throughout the 17th century, Nova Scotia became a focal point of contention between the French and the British, seeking dominance in the North American fur trade. The Treaty of Utrecht in 1713 ceded Nova Scotia to Great Britain, solidifying British control over the region. The British renamed the region "Nova Scotia" (Latin for "New Scotland") to reflect its new identity.

Acadian Expulsion

One of the most tragic chapters in Nova Scotia's history occurred during the mid-18th century. The Acadians, descendants of the French settlers, had established a vibrant community in the region. However, tensions between the British and Acadians led to the infamous Acadian Expulsion of 1755. Thousands of Acadians were forcibly removed from their homes and scattered across the Americas, leaving a lasting impact on Nova Scotia's cultural landscape.

Loyalist Migration and Confederation

The late 18th and early 19th centuries witnessed an influx of Loyalists—Americans who remained loyal to the British Crown during the American Revolution. These Loyalists sought refuge in Nova Scotia, bringing with them their traditions and customs. The diverse cultural heritage of the Loyalists continues to influence the province to this day.

In 1867, Nova Scotia played a pivotal role in the formation of Canada. It was one of the four original provinces to join Confederation, alongside New Brunswick, Ontario, and Quebec. This event marked the beginning of a new chapter in Nova Scotia's history, as it became an integral part of the Canadian federation.

Industrialization and Modernization

As the 19th and 20th centuries progressed, Nova Scotia underwent significant industrialization, particularly in coal mining, shipbuilding, and steel production. Cities like Halifax and Sydney became vital centers of commerce and trade. However, economic challenges and changes in industries also led to periods of hardship, such as the decline of coal mining in the latter half of the 20th century.

Contemporary Nova Scotia

Today, Nova Scotia is a thriving province known for its maritime charm, cultural diversity, and stunning natural beauty. It has become a popular destination for tourism, drawing visitors from around the world to explore its historic sites, coastal landscapes, and vibrant communities.

In recent years, Nova Scotia has seen advancements in various sectors, including technology, healthcare, and education. The province continues to evolve while embracing its rich heritage and preserving its unique traditions.

Climate and Weather

Nova Scotia, located on Canada's eastern coast, is a province renowned for its breathtaking landscapes, maritime heritage, and unique climate. Nestled between the Atlantic Ocean and the Bay of Fundy, Nova Scotia experiences a diverse range of weather patterns throughout the year. This article explores the province's climate and weather, highlighting its distinct seasons and the influence of its coastal geography on meteorological phenomena.

The Four Seasons of Nova Scotia

Nova Scotia experiences a classic four-season climate, each bringing its own charm and activities. Let's delve into what each season has to offer:

Spring (March to May)

As winter gives way to spring, Nova Scotia transforms into a picturesque haven of blooming flowers and lush greenery. The season witnesses gradually warming temperatures, with daytime highs ranging from 5 to 15°C (41 to 59°F). Springtime also brings a mix of rain showers and sunny days, encouraging nature's rejuvenation.

Summer (June to August)

Summer in Nova Scotia is a true delight for locals and visitors alike. Average temperatures reach 20 to 25°C (68 to 77°F), making it ideal for outdoor activities. The coastal breeze provides a refreshing escape from the heat, making it an excellent time to explore the province's pristine beaches and coastal trails.

Autumn (September to November)

As summer fades, Nova Scotia dons a magnificent display of autumn colors. The season brings cooler temperatures, with highs ranging from 10 to 20°C (50 to 68°F). It's the perfect time for leaf peeping, as the province's forests showcase a vibrant tapestry of red, orange, and golden hues.

Winter (December to February)

Winter in Nova Scotia is a wonderland for snow enthusiasts. Average temperatures range from -5 to -1°C (23 to 30°F), creating a snowy paradise for skiing, snowboarding, and other winter sports. The coastal regions experience milder winters due to the tempering effect of the ocean.

Maritime Influence on Weather

Nova Scotia's location along the Atlantic Ocean significantly impacts its weather patterns. The ocean's moderating influence ensures that the province experiences milder winters and cooler summers compared to its continental counterparts. The Bay of Fundy, known for having the highest tides in the world, also affects the weather, creating local variations in climate.

Storms and Nor'easters

Being a coastal region, Nova Scotia is vulnerable to storms and nor'easters, particularly during the fall and winter months. Nor'easters are powerful low-pressure systems that bring strong winds, heavy precipitation, and storm surges, sometimes leading to coastal flooding and erosion. While these storms can be formidable, they also contribute to the province's unique character and its resilient coastal communities.

Climate Change and Adaptation

Like many other regions worldwide, Nova Scotia faces the challenges posed by climate change. Rising sea levels, more intense storms, and shifts in precipitation patterns are some of the issues the province grapples with. In response, Nova Scotia has been proactive in adopting climate change adaptation strategies, including coastal protection measures, sustainable land use planning, and renewable energy initiatives.

Culture

Unraveling the Rich Tapestry of Nova Scotia's Cultural Heritage

Nova Scotia, a picturesque province situated on Canada's eastern coast, is a treasure trove of cultural wonders that have shaped its identity over the centuries. The fusion of Indigenous, European, African, and Acadian influences has resulted in a unique and diverse cultural tapestry. From its vibrant festivals and traditional music to its delectable cuisine and historical landmarks, Nova Scotia's culture offers a captivating journey into the heart of Canada's East Coast.

Indigenous Heritage

Before the arrival of European settlers, Nova Scotia's lands were inhabited by Indigenous peoples, including the Mi'kmaq. Their rich culture and traditions are deeply rooted in the region's history. Today, the Mi'kmaq community plays an essential role in preserving and celebrating their ancestral customs, evident in their powwows, storytelling sessions, and art exhibitions. The significance of Indigenous heritage is also reflected in the names of many towns, rivers, and landmarks across the province.

Acadian Influence

The Acadian culture holds a prominent place in Nova Scotia's identity, with the Acadians establishing their roots in the region during the 17th century. The Acadian descendants have kept their language, music, and culinary traditions alive through generations. Visitors can immerse themselves in the lively Acadian festivals, such as the Tintamarre, which celebrates Acadian National Day, and the Festival, a lively event filled with music, dance, and delicious Acadian cuisine.

Lighthouse Route and Maritime Traditions

Nova Scotia's coastline is dotted with picturesque lighthouses, showcasing the province's strong maritime heritage. The Lighthouse Route, a scenic drive along the South Shore, takes travelers on a journey through fishing villages, sandy beaches, and historic ports. Fishing has been a vital industry for Nova Scotia's, and visitors can experience the maritime way of life by attending fishing derbies, boat races, and exploring the Fisheries Museum of the Atlantic.

4. Celtic and Gaelic Roots

The Scottish and Irish immigrants who settled in Nova Scotia have left an indelible mark on the region's culture. Cape Breton Island, in particular, is renowned for its strong Celtic and Gaelic heritage. Visitors can witness captivating ceilidhs (traditional Gaelic gatherings with music and dance) and witness the breathtaking skill of fiddlers, pipers, and step dancers. The Celtic Colors International Festival is a must-attend event, celebrating Celtic music, arts, and storytelling.

Art and Literature

Nova Scotia has been a source of inspiration for numerous artists and authors, fostering a vibrant creative community. The Art Gallery of Nova Scotia in Halifax showcases a diverse collection of artworks, reflecting the province's cultural diversity. The literary world also finds its place in Nova Scotia, with several renowned authors hailing from the province, and literary festivals attracting book lovers from near and far.

Let's Vacate To
nova scotia

Book Now

20 | Nova Scotia Travel Guide

CHAPTER 1: PLANNING YOUR TRIP

Nova Scotia, with its magnificent coastline, rich history, and dynamic culture, provides visitors with a wide range of activities. Whether you want to explore stunning coastal vistas, learn about maritime history, or indulge in delectable seafood cuisine, Nova Scotia has it all. Follow this thorough guide to arranging your vacation to this lovely Canadian province to ensure you have a memorable and well-organized trip.

When Is the Best Time to Visit?

Nova Scotia has four different seasons, each with its particular beauty. The peak tourist season lasts from late spring to early fall (May to October) when the weather is nice and conducive to outdoor activities. Consider visiting during the shoulder seasons (spring and fall) if you want fewer crowds and reduced lodging rates. Winters can be freezing, but they also offer possibilities for winter sports aficionados as well as the opportunity to attend winter festivals and events.

Making an Itinerary

Nova Scotia has a diverse selection of attractions, including historic sites and national parks, as well as picturesque villages and cultural events. Outline your preferences and interests before planning your schedule. Some must-see locations include:

Visas & Entry Requirements

Nova Scotia, a beautiful province in Canada, draws visitors from all over the world with its breathtaking landscapes, rich culture, and strong economy. If you intend to visit this marine jewel, it is critical to understand the entry criteria and visa laws to ensure smooth and trouble-free travel. This detailed guide will help you through every aspect of entering Nova Scotia.

1. The Visa System in Canada

Canada has a strong and efficient visa system that oversees admission into all of its provinces, including Nova Scotia. Most visitors from other countries must get a visa before entering the country. The Tourist Visa and the Business Visa are the principal visa categories for short-term stays.

2. Visitor Visa to Nova Scotia

If you intend to visit Nova Scotia for leisure, sightseeing, or to see family and friends, you will almost certainly need a Temporary Resident Visa (TRV), often known as a Tourist Visa. To apply for a Tourist Visa, you must go to the closest Canadian embassy or consulate in your native country.

A valid passport, proof of means to sustain your stay, a detailed itinerary, and evidence of ties to your home country are all required during the application process. Before awarding the visa, the Canadian immigration authorities will evaluate your application based on these grounds.

3. Nova Scotia Business Visa

You will need to apply for a Business Visa if your travel to Nova Scotia includes business activities such as attending meetings, conferences, or researching prospective investment possibilities. As with the Tourist Visa, you must apply to the Canadian embassy or consulate in your native country.

A letter of invitation from a Canadian company or organization with which you intend to do business is usually required for the Business Visa application procedure. You'll also need to show that you have enough money to cover your stay and that you intend to return to your native country when your visa expires.

4. eTA (Electronic Travel Authorization)

Some visitors, such as nationals of visa-exempt nations, may not need a visa to visit Canada. Even if their final destination is Nova Scotia, individuals must get an Electronic Travel Authorization (eTA) before boarding their aircraft to Canada.

The eTA is an electronically linked travel authorization that is required for travelers from countries that do not require a visa. To avoid last-minute problems, apply for an eTA well in advance of your travel dates.

5. International Students and Contractors

If you intend to study or work in Nova Scotia, you will need permission in addition to the regular Tourist or Business Visa. International students must get a Study

Permit, whereas temporary workers must seek a Work Permit. These permits each have their own set of qualifying requirements and application procedures.

6. Renewals and Extensions

If your circumstances change while in Nova Scotia and you want to extend your stay or change your visa status, you must apply for an extension or renewal before your present permit expires. Late applications may result in penalties or difficulties in acquiring subsequent licenses.

Budgeting

Calculate your vacation costs, including lodging, transportation, meals, activities, and mementos. To save money on famous attractions, consider purchasing attraction passes or discount cards. It's also a good idea to bring extra cash with you because not all locations take credit cards.

Transportation: The first step is to get to Nova Scotia. If you're traveling from afar, examine flight prices from various airlines and try reserving ahead of time to achieve lower rates. Once in the province, look into several modes of transportation, such as rental automobiles, public buses, and ride-sharing programs. Carpooling can be a cost-effective way to get around and experience the region if you're traveling in a group.

Accommodation: Nova Scotia has a variety of lodging options, ranging from opulent hotels to budget-friendly hostels and comfortable bed & breakfasts. Consider vacationing in smaller villages near popular attractions rather than in the middle of a bustling metropolis to save money. Additionally, using travel comparison websites might assist you in finding the best discounts on lodging.

Dining: While sampling local food is an important part of any trip experience, eating out for every meal can rapidly add up. Choose a combination of local cafes and self-catering to keep your meal costs in check. Visiting local markets to buy fresh vegetables and snacks not only saves money but also allows you to engage with locals and taste the authentic flavors of Nova Scotia.

Free and Low-Cost Activities: Nova Scotia is blessed with a wealth of natural beauty, and many of its attractions are free or only for a small fee. Visit stunning national parks, picturesque trails, clean beaches, and quaint fishing villages without breaking the budget. Attend local events and festivals to immerse yourself in the region's lively culture.

Entertainment and Sightseeing: While in Nova Scotia, you might wish to take advantage of certain paid activities and attractions. Look for discounted passes or combination tickets that allow you to visit many locations for a lower cost. Travel during the shoulder seasons, when many tourist attractions offer discounted fees.

Travel in a Group: If possible, travel with friends or family to split expenses such as lodging, transportation, and food. Splitting expenses might make your trip cheaper and allow you to share the experience.

Travel Insurance: It's always a good idea to purchase travel insurance to protect yourself from unexpected expenses like medical crises or trip cancellations. Compare various insurance carriers to get a plan that meets your needs and fits within your budget.

Packing Tips for a Fantastic Vacation
1. Weather-Responsive Clothing
Nova Scotia has a wide range of weather conditions, so pack appropriately. Summers can be lovely, but bring clothing because temperatures can change. Pack lightweight attire, such as t-shirts, shorts, and sundresses, as well as a light jacket or sweater for chilly evenings. Temperatures are pleasant in the fall and spring, so carry layers and a waterproof jacket. Bring a large winter coat, warm sweaters, scarves, gloves, and insulated boots because winter temperatures can be frigid.

2. Comfortable Footwear
Exploring Nova Scotia's natural attractions and attractive communities requires comfortable footwear. Bring durable hiking boots for outdoor adventures, flip-flops or sandals for beach days, and comfortable walking shoes for city exploration.

3. Outdoor Requirements
If you plan to go on hikes or outdoor trips, bring a daypack with you to carry water, snacks, a map, and a camera. Bring

sunscreen, insect repellent, and a wide-brimmed hat to protect yourself from the sun and annoying insects.

4. Swimsuits

Because Nova Scotia has so many gorgeous beaches and lakes, bringing swimwear is essential, especially during the summer months. Even if you don't intend to swim, you could be enticed to cool off in the water on a hot day.

5. Travel Documents and Needs

Check that you have all of the relevant travel documentation, such as your passport, identification, and any applicable visas. It's a good idea to preserve both digital and physical copies of vital documents, as well as the contact information for your embassy or consulate. Pack any necessary medications, a first-aid kit, and travel insurance for peace of mind.

Photography Equipment Nova Scotia's magnificent landscapes and attractive villages provide numerous opportunities for stunning shots. Bring additional batteries, memory cards, and a tripod to capture the essence of this enthralling place.

Chargers and Adapters

Canada has a different electrical sockets and voltage, so bring the necessary adapters and chargers for your electronic gadgets.

Reusable Water Bottle

Carry a reusable water bottle with you on your travels to stay hydrated. Nova Scotia has an abundance of freshwater sources, and this modest eco-friendly measure will aid in the reduction of plastic trash.

Cash and credit cards are accepted.

While larger cities and towns accept credit cards, it's always a good idea to keep extra cash on hand for little transactions or if you travel to more distant places.

Daily Requirements

Bring your regular toiletries, such as shampoo, conditioner, toothbrush, and a towel. Because the tap water in Nova Scotia is safe to drink, a refillable water bottle is sufficient.

CHAPTER 2: EXPLORING THE BEAUTY OF NOVA SCOTIA

A Journey through Its Historical Places

Nova Scotia, Canada's seaside province, is rich in history and culture. This picturesque region is rich in fascinating stories of exploration, settlement, and battle, and it is home to countless historical landmarks that remain as testaments to its rich history. Let's take a riveting tour around Nova Scotia's historical places, from ancient indigenous sites to colonial forts and lighthouses, where each destination tells a unique chapter in the province's illustrious history.

1. Louisburg Fortress

The Fortress of Louisburg, one of Canada's most significant historical landmarks, provides tourists with a look at 18th-century colonial life. This restored French stronghold looms towering on Cape Breton Island's eastern shore. It was once a bustling commercial town and military stronghold, but now it provides immersive living history experiences, guided tours, and exciting reenactments that transport tourists back to the New France era.

2. National Historic Site of Grand-Pré

Grand-Pré, a UNESCO World Heritage Site, commemorates the terrible deportation of the Acadians in the mid-18th century. The beautiful gardens and evocative sculptures at the site tell the story of the Acadian community and their difficulties during expulsion, making it a heartbreaking and thought-provoking destination for history buffs.

3. Lighthouse at Peggy's Cove

The Peggy's Cove Lighthouse, perched on the rocky cliffs of St. Margaret's Bay, is one of Nova Scotia's most photographed and recognizable sights. This charming lighthouse, which was built in 1868, continues to direct ships safely along the shore. The nearby fishing village, with its vividly painted cottages, adds to the appeal of this historical site.

4. Kejimkujik National Park

While it is well-known for its natural beauty, Kejimkujik National Park also has important historical significance. The park contains a large number of Mi'kmaq petroglyphs, which are rock sculptures carved into the terrain by indigenous peoples thousands of years ago. These petroglyphs offer a look into the Mi'kmaq Nation's rich cultural legacy.

5. National Historic Site of Alexander Graham Bell

This memorial honors Alexander Graham Bell, the famed inventor of the telephone, and is located in the picturesque village of Baddeck. The museum displays relics, models, and interactive exhibits that highlight Bell's significant scientific discoveries as well as his deep connection to the region.

6. Joggins Fossil Cliffs

For those interested in ancient history, the Joggins Fossil Cliffs provide a unique opportunity to study Nova Scotia's geological treasures. This UNESCO World Heritage Site is home to a plethora of fossils, including some of the world's earliest terrestrial vertebrates, which provide unique insights into life on Earth 300 million years ago.

7. Annapolis Royal Historic Gardens

At the Annapolis Royal Historic Gardens, you may immerse yourself in Nova Scotia's historic past. These finely planned gardens showcase the province's horticultural legacy while providing a look into the daily lives of early inhabitants. Visitors can explore historical structures, period gardens, and instructive exhibits that bring history to life.

Museums & Art Galleries: Cultural Heritage

Nova Scotia, located on Canada's east coast, is a treasure trove of artistic legacy that draws art and history enthusiasts equally. The province, which has a rich cultural tapestry, is home to a broad array of museums and art galleries that highlight the creative energy and historical significance of the region. There is something for everyone to explore and appreciate, from contemporary art places to historical organizations.

1. Nova Scotia Art Gallery

The Art Gallery of Nova Scotia, located in Halifax, the provincial capital, is a must-see for art lovers. This prestigious institution houses a large collection of Canadian and foreign art, including works by well-known Nova Scotian painters. The gallery offers a complete trip through many artistic trends and periods, from paintings and sculptures to photography and decorative arts.

2. The Atlantic Maritime Museum

The Maritime Museum of the Atlantic in Halifax goes beyond traditional art to capture the province's deep relationship to the water. Visitors can see fascinating marine-themed art, ship models, and relics that highlight the province's maritime heritage, shipbuilding prowess, and storied seafaring customs.

3. The Ross Creek Arts Centre

Ross Creek Centre for the Arts is a tranquil retreat for artists and art fans alike, nestled among the magnificent landscapes of Canning. Exhibitions, artist residencies, seminars, and performances are held at this creative retreat, which fosters an environment of artistic growth and cultural interchange.

4. Cape Breton Craft and Design Centre

This facility, located on the beautiful island of Cape Breton, honors the region's rich craft traditions. Visitors can marvel at a plethora of locally handmade ceramics, textiles, jewelry, and other handcrafted products that capture the soul of Cape Breton's artistic past.

5. Hector Heritage Quay

The Hector ancestry Quay in Pictou, Nova Scotia, provides a unique view into the province's Scottish ancestry. This interactive museum tells the narrative of Scottish immigration to Nova Scotia, documenting their difficulties and achievements via interesting exhibits and artwork.

6. Lunenburg Art Gallery

The Lunenburg Art Gallery, steeped in coastal charm, exhibits the works of local artists and crafters. This community-oriented gallery fosters artistic talent while conserving the region's creative past.

7. Yarmouth County Museum and documents

Take a historical journey to the Yarmouth County Museum and Archives, which displays an intriguing mix of art, artifacts, and documents reflecting the area's cultural background. The museum is home to paintings, sculptures, and historical artifacts that vividly depict Yarmouth's past.

8. Mary E. Black Gallery

This contemporary craft gallery in the center of Halifax is dedicated to promoting craft as an art form. Visitors can explore thought-provoking exhibits, participate in workshops, and learn about the ever-changing world of contemporary craft.

9. Coastal Region of Peggy's Cove

While not a museum or gallery in the traditional sense, the Peggy's Cove Coastal Region has inspired innumerable artists throughout the years. Visitors can take in the stunning coastal scenery preserved on canvases and pictures, generating a sense of creative serenity.

The museums and art galleries in Nova Scotia provide an enthralling blend of historical relevance, cultural history, and modern creativity. These institutions and cultural sites give an enriching and fascinating experience in the heart of Canada's dynamic east coast, whether you're an art fan, a history buff, or simply looking for inspiration.

Let's Vacate To
nova scotia

Coastal Region of Peggy's Cove

Book Now

38 | Nova Scotia Travel Guide

CHAPTER 3: FOOD AND DINING

Exploring Local Cuisine and Specialties

Nova Scotia's cuisine offers a culinary journey that reflects its history and maritime traditions, with a distinct blend of fresh seafood, locally sourced ingredients, and cultural influences.

1. Extravaganza of Seafood

The coastline of Nova Scotia runs for thousands of kilometers, making it a seafood lover's dream. Lobster, scallops, clams, and haddock are just a few of the sea riches included on the menu. A typical Maritime lobster boil or delicious scallops cooked to perfection are available.

2. Scallops Digby

Digby, located on the Bay of Fundy, is famous for its world-class scallops. These sweet and soft morsels are frequently pan-seared with a light seasoning, allowing their inherent tastes to show. Every year, the Digby Scallop Festival honors these treasures, attracting foodies from all over.

3. Hodge Podge

Hodge Podge is a typical Nova Scotian vegetable meal that highlights the region's wealth. A variety of fresh summer veggies, including peas, carrots, young potatoes, and beans, are simply seasoned and cooked together. It's a beautiful celebration of the local crop and a summertime classic.

4. Apples from the Annapolis Valley

The lush soil and temperature of the Annapolis Valley make it an ideal location for apple farming. These fruits, ranging from crisp and luscious McIntosh apples to versatile Cortland's, are used in everything from pies and crisps to cider and apple-based savory dishes.

5. Blueberry Grunt

Blueberries grow wild in Nova Scotia, and residents have perfected the technique of turning them into the Blueberry Grunt, a cozy dessert. Cooked with sugar and spices, these juicy berries are topped with dumplings that steam and "grunt" as they cook. It's a taste of the rustic charm of Nova Scotia.

6. Donair

Nova Scotia's variation on the popular street dish, the donair, is distinctive. It's a late-night favorite and a monument to the province's wide culinary options, a pita wrap packed with seasoned and sliced spiced beef, chopped tomatoes, onions, and a sweet garlic sauce.

7. Pudding from Lunenburg

This traditional steamed delicacy, named after the scenic town of Lunenburg, contains molasses, brown sugar, and breadcrumbs. It's a warming treat with a history dating back to the province's seafaring days.

Top Restaurants and Cafés for Culinary Delights

Nova Scotia, Canada's maritime treasure, is well-known not only for its beautiful coastal vistas and rich history but also for its dynamic culinary scene. Nova Scotia offers a pleasant gourmet experience for visitors and locals alike, with a blend of fresh seafood, locally produced products, and a creative culinary attitude. In this post, we will take you on a virtual tour of some of the best restaurants and cafés in Nova Scotia that you should not miss when visiting.

1. Dartmouth is the location of The Canteen.

The Canteen is a hidden treasure in Dartmouth that offers a trendy and refined dining experience. Chef Renée Lavallée adds a modern twist to classic recipes while highlighting locally produced ingredients. The Canteen is a must-visit for those looking for a refined yet approachable culinary excursion, serving everything from scrumptious seafood to mouthwatering sweets.

Agricola Street Brasserie is located in Halifax.

Agricola Street Brasserie is a true farm-to-table experience, known for its welcoming environment and commitment to using locally sourced vegetables. The menu changes with the seasons to ensure that diners enjoy the freshest ingredients available in Nova Scotia. The Brasserie's commitment to environmentally friendly dining methods has earned it a particular place in the hearts of foodies.

3. Location of Five Fishermen Restaurant: Halifax

The Five Fishermen Restaurant, housed in a historic building, is a seafood lover's dream. The menu features a selection of dishes that honor the wealth of the sea, with a focus on Atlantic seafood. This restaurant is great for special occasions or a memorable night out due to its exquisite decor and professional service.

4. Lane's Privateer Inn is located in Liverpool.

Lane's Privateer Inn in Liverpool is a must-see for a taste of maritime heritage and great eating. The restaurant of the inn serves a mix of traditional and contemporary cuisine, with a focus on locally caught fish. Enjoy a wonderful supper while learning about the region's rich maritime past.

5. Location of the Lunenburg Arms Restaurant: Lunenburg

The Lunenburg Arms Restaurant, located in the picturesque village of Lunenburg, provides a comfortable and inviting atmosphere. The menu features a wide range of meals crafted using locally sourced ingredients that capture the essence of Nova Scotia's culinary tradition. This restaurant offers a great gastronomic trip whether you're having a full brunch or a romantic night.

Cafés: 1. Two if By Sea Café, Dartmouth and Halifax

Two if By Sea Café has become a favorite among coffee connoisseurs for its superb pastries and gourmet coffee. With its lovely seaside locations, this café provides a tranquil setting to enjoy a cup of coffee and scrumptious snacks.

2. The Nook Espresso Bar & Lounge (Halifax)

The Nook Espresso Bar & Lounge is a quaint and attractive café that is a coffee lover's paradise. Their attention to creating the perfect cup of coffee, as well as a menu of light nibbles and desserts, make it an ideal place to unwind and recharge.

3. Good Luck Café Location: Halifax

Café Good Luck is a quirky and pleasant ambiance that embodies Halifax's artistic spirit. This café is popular among locals looking for a wonderful escape because of its distinctive beverages and exquisite baked pastries.

Seafood Sensations: Because of its proximity to the coast, Nova Scotia is a seafood lover's heaven. Succulent lobster, soft scallops, abundant mussels, and the legendary Digby clams are on the menu. The seafood here is unrivaled in freshness and flavor, whether savored in a simple lobster roll or delicately prepared in a fine dining institution.

Acadian Influences: The Acadian legacy is firmly ingrained in the gastronomic scene of Nova Scotia. Traditional Acadian comfort foods like "Rappie Pie," prepared with grated potatoes and pork, represent the province's French history. Don't miss out on other Acadian delicacies like "Lobster à la française" and "Pâté à la viande."

Farm-to-Table Treasures: The rich landscapes of Nova Scotia generate an abundance of locally grown produce. The province's farm-to-table movement ensures that tourists can experience fresh and seasonal ingredients in every mouthful, from crisp apples in the Annapolis Valley to brilliant berries along the Cabot Trail.

Iconic Blueberry Dishes: Nova Scotia is well-known for its wild blueberries. These antioxidant-rich berries can be found in pies and jams, as well as pancakes and sweets. For a true flavor of Nova Scotia, try a slice of homemade blueberry pie or a stack of blueberry pancakes topped with maple syrup.

Craft Beverages: The craft beverage market in the province is growing, with a varied choice of cocktails to satisfy every palate. Explore the Tidal Bay Wine Route, where you can sip crisp white wines that have been specially designed to match the region's seafood.

Tidal Bay Appellation: Tidal Bay is the world's first and only appellation for a wine style, and it is located in Nova Scotia. This white wine is distinguished by its sharp acidity and ability to complement the province's seafood offers. Tidal Bay wines are a true expression of the terroir and coastal impact of Nova Scotia.

Traditional Nova Scotian Poutine: The province offers its version of poutine, which includes hand-cut fries, delicious gravy, and local cheese curds, as a Nova Scotian spin on the famous Canadian comfort meal. Some varieties incorporate lobster or pulled pork toppings for added decadence.

CHAPTER 4: NIGHTLIFE AND ENTERTAINMENT

Exploring Activities and Entertainment

Nova Scotia, located on Canada's east coast, is known for its compelling blend of natural beauty, maritime history, and a thriving cultural environment. There is no shortage of activities and entertainment opportunities for locals and visitors alike, from quaint seaside villages to breathtaking vistas. Nova Scotia has something for everyone, whether you're an outdoor enthusiast, a history buff, or an art lover.

1. Coastal Excursions

The mountainous coastline of Nova Scotia stretches for almost 5,000 miles, providing numerous opportunities for outdoor excursions. Hikers can follow trails that zigzag through lush forests, rolling hills, and stunning cliffs. The Cabot Trail, for example, gives breathtaking views as it passes through the Cape Breton Highlands, while the Peggy's Cove Coastal Trail offers an amazing journey along rocky coasts.

2. Waterfront Treats

Given its nautical background, Nova Scotia's waterfront regions are alive and well. The waterfront in Halifax, with its iconic waterfront boardwalk, has a variety of shops, restaurants, and activities. Explore the scenic bays and inlets by taking a walk, taking a harbor cruise, or renting a kayak.

3. Cultural Inclusion

Nova Scotia has various museums and heritage places to explore for individuals interested in history and culture. With its military reenactments and interactive exhibitions, the Halifax Citadel National Historic Site transports you to the nineteenth century. The Maritime Museum of the Atlantic displays artifacts from the Titanic disaster as well as the province's seafaring history.

4. Festivals and Special Events

Throughout the year, Nova Scotia holds several festivals and events. The Halifax International Busker Festival attracts street performers from all over the world, while the Celtic Colors International Festival promotes Celtic music and culture throughout the island. The Nova Scotia

Multicultural Festival celebrates the variety of the province via music, dance, and food.

5. Culinary Delights

Foodies will enjoy Nova Scotia's culinary scene, which is heavily inspired by the province's maritime environment. From delicious lobster to savory scallops, indulge in freshly caught seafood. Taste gourmet cheeses, handcrafted jams, and fresh produce at local farmers' markets.

6. Entertainment and Art

The art scene in Nova Scotia is growing, with galleries and studios displaying a varied range of works. The Art Gallery of Nova Scotia exhibits both local and international art, while the Ross Creek Centre for the Arts hosts workshops and exhibitions in a scenic rural environment.

7. Beach Vacations

Nova Scotia is an attractive beach vacation destination because of its numerous sandy beaches. Spend a leisurely day at Lawrence town Beach sunning and swimming, or explore the dunes at Martinique Beach Provincial Park.

8. Whale Observation

The Bay of Fundy, noted for having the world's highest tides, also provides superb whale viewing possibilities. Take a boat excursion to see humpback, minke, and fin whales, as well as dolphins and porpoises.

9. Nightlife and Music

The music culture in Nova Scotia is thriving, with live performances ranging from traditional folk music to current indie bands. Halifax has a vibrant nightlife with various clubs, pubs, and live music venues where you can relax and dance the night away.

Nova Scotia's distinct combination of natural wonders, cultural experiences, and recreational opportunities makes it an excellent location for anybody looking for a memorable and rewarding vacation. Nova Scotia has something to offer that will captivate your senses and leave you with lasting memories, whether you are drawn to its environmental beauty, historical significance, artistic manifestations, or just its friendly welcome.

A Haven for Outdoor Enthusiasts

Nova Scotia, located on Canada's east coast, is a refuge for outdoor lovers looking for magnificent scenery and exhilarating activities. This region, with its craggy coastline, gorgeous lakes, and lush woods, offers a variety of outdoor activities for any sort of adventurer. Whether you enjoy hiking, water activities, or wildlife, Nova Scotia has something wonderful in store for you.

[Hiking Adventures: Discovering Nature's Glory](#)

Hiking paths in Nova Scotia are a dream come true for individuals who find tranquility amid nature. The province offers a broad assortment of trails ideal for all levels, from beginner-friendly roads to demanding climbs for experienced trekkers.

1. Cape Chignecto Coastal walk: This Fundy Footpath walk offers a multi-day hike along towering cliffs overlooking the Bay of Fundy. It's a true endurance test that rewards hikers with panoramic vistas and the opportunity to experience the world's highest tides.

2. Cape Breton Highlands National Park: Home to the well-known Skyline Trail, this park allows visitors to stroll through rich Acadian woodlands and along breathtaking coastal cliffs. The views of the Gulf of St. Lawrence are breathtaking.

3. Kejimkujik National Park: This Park is ideal for a combination of trekking and paddling. You may discover both land and water beauty on pathways that wind through old woodlands and along lovely lakeshores.

Kayaking & Canoeing in Paradise

The waters of Nova Scotia provide a playground for kayakers and canoeists. The province's aquatic beauties offer a wonderful experience, whether you're gliding across quiet lakes or navigating the mild rapids of meandering rivers.

1. Back Harbor of Lunenburg: Paddle around the colorful UNESCO World Heritage town of Lunenburg, discovering secret coves and old architecture from a new perspective.

2. St. Mary's River: This River offers a tranquil journey through beautiful surroundings, quiet waters, and wildlife viewing chances. It's an excellent choice for beginners and families.

3. **Bras D'Or Lake**: This large saltwater lake, known as Canada's inland sea, provides a spectacular backdrop for kayakers. It's a heaven for paddlers looking for peace, with various bays and islands to explore.

Whale Watching: Marvel at Majestic Giants

The coastline of Nova Scotia is famous for its diverse marine life, and whale watching is an absolute must for visitors hoping to witness these spectacular creatures.

1. **The Bay of Fundy**: known for its high tides and rich marine habitats, provides a unique opportunity to see whales such as humpbacks, minke whales, and even the rare North Atlantic right whale.

2. **Brier Island:** This is a popular place for whale watching, especially in the summer and fall. Take a guided boat tour and look out for stunning breaches and tail flips.

3. **Digby Neck's nutrient-rich waters:** this attract a diverse range of marine species, making it a great place to see not only whales but also seals, dolphins, and seabirds.

The outdoor activities available in Nova Scotia are as varied as its surroundings. This province delivers an outdoor adventure of a lifetime, whether you're climbing hikes, canoeing on beautiful waters, or gazing at the majesty of marine giants. So pack your belongings, immerse yourself in nature, and prepare to make memories that will last a lifetime in this Canadian outdoor paradise.

Festivals, Museums, and Historic Sites

Nova Scotia, located on Canada's eastern coast, is a province rich in cultural activities that highlight its history, customs, and lively community spirit. Nova Scotia has a broad assortment of cultural activities for both locals and visitors to enjoy, ranging from exciting festivals that showcase the province's musical and creative talents to world-class museums and historic monuments that offer an insight into its past. Let's have a look at some of the most enthralling cultural events Nova Scotia has to offer:

1. Festivals

The festivals of Nova Scotia reflect the provinces vibrant and diversified cultural environment. Throughout the year, the province conducts a variety of events that reflect various facets of its legacy. The Halifax International Busker Festival is one of the most renowned festivals, where streets come alive with street performers, artists, and musicians from all over the world, capturing audiences with their extraordinary talents. The Celtic Colors International Festival** honors Nova Scotia's Scottish and Celtic heritage with a week-long celebration of song, dance, and cultural events set against the breathtaking backdrop of autumn leaves.

2. Museums

Nova Scotia's museums take visitors on an interactive tour through its history and culture. The **Nova Scotia Museum** network includes several locations throughout the province, notably the Maritime Museum of the Atlantic in Halifax. This museum provides an enthralling overview of the province's marine legacy, with displays on shipwrecks, the Titanic, and Halifax's historic role as a major port city. The **Art Gallery of Nova Scotia** exhibits a diverse selection of artworks by local and international artists, allowing visitors to gain insight into the province's artistic evolution.

3. Historic Places

Historic places in Nova Scotia provide a window into the past for history buffs. Fort Anne National Historic Site near Annapolis Royal is one of Canada's oldest national historic sites, offering insight into the region's colonial past through well-preserved fortifications and educational displays. The Grand-Pré National Historic Site, which recalls the Acadian people and their sad exodus from the area in the 18th century, is another highlight. The landscapes and sculptures at the site evoke the emotional journey of the Acadian people.

4. Route of the Lighthouse

The Lighthouse Route along the South Shore is a must-see for a gorgeous excursion through both natural beauty and history. This picturesque route features charming fishing villages, a craggy coastline, and, of course, iconic lighthouses. The Peggy's Cove Lighthouse, built on granite rocks overlooking the Atlantic Ocean, is one of the most well-known sights. Because of its gorgeous environment, it has been a popular subject for artists and photographers.

Discovering Regional Cuisine and Seafood Delights

Exploring Nova Scotia's culinary scene, which is strongly based on the region's history, culture, and availability of some of the freshest seafood on the globe, is one of the most exciting elements of visiting the province. Take a culinary trip across Nova Scotia's picturesque villages and lively cities to explore an array of local cuisine and seafood delicacies that will leave your taste buds begging for more.

1. A Seafood Connoisseur's Paradise

The coastline of Nova Scotia runs for thousands of kilometers, and its proximity to the water has made seafood an essential aspect of its cuisine. From luscious lobster to plump scallops, and from juicy mussels to flawlessly grilled fish, seafood lovers have plenty of alternatives. The fishing settlements of the province offer a true taste of coastal life, and the seafood here is more than simply a meal - it's an experience.

2. The Culinary Heritage

Nova Scotia's culinary tradition is inextricably linked to its Indigenous beginnings, European settlements, and various immigrant communities. Traditional Acadian delicacies such as 'Rappie Pie,' a robust casserole consisting of grated potatoes and meat, are available, as are Scottish-inspired haggis and the strong tastes of Irish stews. These influences combine to provide a one-of-a-kind blend of flavors that convey the story of Nova Scotia's past.

3. Visiting Farmers' Markets

Exploring the farmers' markets is a must for an authentic flavor of local Nova Scotian ingredients. For example, the Halifax Seaport Farmers' Market is a thriving cluster of local producers selling everything from fresh vegetables and artisanal cheeses to homemade preserves and baked delicacies. Engaging with farmers and craftspeople not only gives you insight into the region's culinary landscape but also helps local businesses.

4. Dining with a View at the Lighthouse

The coastline of Nova Scotia is lined with gorgeous lighthouses, some of which have been converted into charming dining businesses. Imagine enjoying a scrumptious seafood feast while gazing out at the huge Atlantic Ocean, with the relaxing murmur of waves in the background. This one-of-a-kind dining experience blends culinary pleasures with gorgeous scenery to create an unforgettable supper.

5. The Taste of Nova Scotian Lobster

Lobster is a major draw in Nova Scotia's culinary scene. Along the seaside, lobster pounds and seafood shacks serve the freshest and most succulent lobsters you've ever tasted. Whether you want it steamed, butter-poached, or in a creamy lobster roll, sampling Nova Scotia's lobster is a must-do on any gastronomic trip here.

6. Coastal Flavors & Foraging

The various landscapes of Nova Scotia provide a plethora of wild ingredients just waiting to be discovered. Explore the coastal regions and forests on guided foraging tours, harvesting delicious treasures such as seaweed, wild berries, and herbs. Incorporating these distinct flavors into your dishes offers a degree of authenticity and connection to the place.

Artisan's Haven: Celebrating the Creative Spirit of Nova Scotia

Nova Scotia has long been a shelter for artists and crafters, who are inspired by its rocky coastline, historic sites, and rich cultural heritage. The province is home to a plethora of art galleries, studios, and craft fairs where local artists can present their work. Visitors can watch the creative process firsthand, interact with artists, and take home one-of-a-kind pieces that capture the spirit of Nova Scotia.

Nautical-Themed Crafts: Maritime Influences

It's no surprise that nautical-themed crafts are popular in Nova Scotia, given its maritime history and magnificent coastline. These crafts, which range from finely carved wooden ships to hand-painted lighthouse sculptures, represent the province's deep affinity to the water. Nautical souvenirs are both attractive reminders of the region's seafaring history and delightful gifts that appeal to both locals and tourists.

Traditional Textile Crafts: Bringing History and Modernity Together

Textile crafts in Nova Scotia combine ancient techniques with modern patterns. Rug hooking, quilting, and knitting have a long tradition in the area, with craftsmen using locally obtained materials to create creations that ooze warmth and authenticity. These crafts are not only utilitarian, but they also carry stories from previous generations, making them treasured keepsakes and gifts.

Culinary Delights: Edible Gifts

For those who want to bring a taste of Nova Scotia home, culinary souvenirs are a wonderful way to do so. These items, ranging from maple-infused snacks to locally created jams and preserves, provide a literal taste of Nova Scotia. Food and beverage mementos not only honor the region's culinary heritage but also make practical and delightful gifts that may be enjoyed long after the trip has ended.

Indigenous Art and Crafts: Celebrating First Nations Culture

Indigenous groups with strong artistic traditions can be found in Nova Scotia. Indigenous art and crafts express a strong connection to the land, spirituality, and ancestors. Traditional beadwork, basketry, and sculptures feature elaborate motifs and bright colors with cultural significance. Purchasing Indigenous artists' work is a meaningful approach to acknowledging and respecting the province's rich heritage.

Contemporary Crafts: Contemporary Takes on Traditional Crafts

While Nova Scotia values its heritage, the local art community welcomes modernity as well. Contemporary artisans frequently mix ancient crafts with innovative processes, resulting in pieces that bridge the past and the present. These one-of-a-kind masterpieces appeal to a wide range of tastes, making them excellent choices for personal keepsakes as well as thoughtful gifts.

Beautiful Souvenirs & Gifts from Enchanting Nova Scotia

Nova Scotia is a treasure trove of unique souvenirs and presents that capture the heart of this enchanting Canadian province, with its rocky coastlines, rich maritime heritage, and vibrant culture. Whether you're a visitor searching for souvenirs to remember your trip or a local looking for thoughtful gifts, Nova Scotia has a variety of selections that charmingly reflect the province's charm and character.

1. Handmade Nautical Treats

It's no wonder that Nova Scotia has a large assortment of nautical-themed souvenirs given its rich marine background. These crafts, which range from finely carved wooden ships to hand-painted lighthouses, not only create beautiful display pieces but also reflect the tale of the province's naval heritage.

2. Lobster-Inspired Design

Lobster is a culinary delight as well as a pillar of Nova Scotia's fisheries industry. Souvenirs featuring lobsters include lobster-shaped keychains, porcelain plates, and even lobster claw bottle openers. These things are a unique and entertaining way to remember your stay in the province.

3. Sweet Maple Treats

Because maple trees abound in Nova Scotia, maple products are popular among both natives and tourists. Maple syrup, maple candies, and maple-infused foods are not only delicious, but they also taste like the natural sweetness of the region.

4. Crafts Inspired by the Celts

Nova Scotia, which has a significant Scottish background, celebrates its Celtic roots via numerous arts and crafts. Celtic jewelry, tartan scarves, and even bagpipes can be found here. These goods honor the province's historical connections and are thoughtful gifts.

5. Pottery and artisanal crafts

Local craftsmen in Nova Scotia create beautiful pottery, ceramics, and crafts that highlight the province's beautiful scenery and culture. From hand-painted tiles depicting coastal scenery to hand-thrown mugs with elaborate designs, these objects reflect the local artisans' creativity and talent.

6. Genuine Mi'kmaq Crafts

Nova Scotia's indigenous Mi'kmaq people have a rich cultural legacy. Their traditional crafts, including as elaborate beadwork, quillwork, and dreamcatchers, provide a one-of-a-kind and meaningful way to interact with the indigenous culture and bring a piece of their heritage home.

7. Home Decor Inspired by the Sea

Nova Scotia's harsh coastline beauty is frequently represented in home decor products such as driftwood sculptures, sea glass jewelry, and seashell-adorned picture frames. These pieces bring the tranquillity of the ocean into every living space.

Exploring Charming Nova Scotia's Bars and Pubs

In the middle of this beautiful setting, the province has a bustling and diversified bar and pub scene that appeals to both locals and visitors. If you're looking for a quaint pub with a historic feel, a vibrant bar with live music, or a waterfront restaurant with stunning views, Nova Scotia has something for everyone.

1. Old Port Pub and Grill

The Old Port Pub & Grill, located in ancient Lunenburg, captures the sense of nautical tradition. With its rustic design, wooden beams, and nautical influences, this tavern oozes warmth in a wonderful structure. While taking in the view of the bustling waterfront, enjoy a range of local craft brews, fresh seafood, and traditional pub foods.

2. The Split Crow Public House

For decades, Halifax's Split Crow Pub has been a fixture on the local bar scene. It's popular with locals and tourists alike, thanks to live music, an enormous choice of beers on tap, and a lively ambiance. The memorabilia-adorned walls and the upbeat atmosphere make for a memorable night out.

3. The Red Shoe Public House

The Red Shoe Pub in Mabou, Cape Breton, is owned by the famed Rankin family and offers a unique blend of music, culture, and hospitality. Traditional Celtic music performances and a warm atmosphere make for a pleasant experience. While sipping a pint of local beer, tap your feet to the beat of traditional sounds.

4. The Henry Residence

The Henry House, a historic jewel in Halifax, mixes a classic pub ambiance with a touch of sophistication. This bar, housed in a 19th-century building, provides an excellent assortment of specialty beers, a wide menu, and an appealing fireplace, ideal for chilly Nova Scotian evenings.

5. Nooks and cranny

The Nook and Cranny in Truro is known for its modern, urban-industrial ambiance. This bar is a favorite among the younger generation, with an ever-changing array of specialty brews and creative cuisine. It's a hotspot for inventive flavors, from gourmet burgers to artisanal cocktails.

6. Dockside Bar and Grill

The Dockside Bar & Grill, located in the historic town of Shelburne, offers stunning waterfront vistas as well as a scrumptious seafood-focused menu. The big outdoor patio with a view of the port is the ideal place to unwind and enjoy the marine environment.

7. The Brewing Company of the Church

The Church Brewing Company, located in a refurbished church in Wolf Ville, flawlessly integrates history with current craft brewing. This one-of-a-kind establishment serves a variety of house-brewed beers as well as a menu incorporating locally produced products. The atmosphere is nothing short of divine.

8. The Snug Public House

The Snug Pub, located in the lovely town of Pictou, is a peaceful haven with a rich nautical past. It's a terrific place to unwind after seeing the town's historic sights, thanks to its wooden interior, traditional decor, and a broad range of beers.

Nova Scotia's bars and pubs appeal to a wide range of interests and preferences, from bustling waterfront establishments to ancient pubs with stories to tell. Whether you're a native looking for a familiar hangout or a visitor eager to experience Nova Scotia's distinct spirit, these places offer more than simply drinks - they provide a window into the province's heart and soul.

Performances and live music

Nova Scotia, located on Canada's east coast, is known for its gorgeous landscapes, rich history, and dynamic cultural scene. Nova Scotia, with its rolling hills, charming fishing villages, and dramatic coastlines, also has a strong live music and performance culture that appeals to both locals and visitors. The province offers a varied range of musical experiences that captivate the hearts of everyone who listen, from traditional Celtic tunes to modern indie bands.

1. Maritime Melodies and Celtic Roots

Nova Scotia has rich cultural roots, with a heritage that is closely linked to its Celtic and Acadian predecessors. Traditional music brings this history to life, and there are plenty of opportunities to appreciate the soul-stirring tunes that have been passed down through centuries. Local bars and taverns frequently hold live sessions with fiddles, bagpipes, and accordions, resulting in an intimate and authentic ambiance reminiscent of the region's Celtic roots.

2. Extravaganzas at Festivals

Throughout the year, Nova Scotia organizes a slew of music festivals catering to a wide range of tastes and genres. The Stan Rogers Folk Festival in Canso is a well-known gathering of folk, roots, and acoustic musicians from around the world. The Halifax Jazz Festival, for those who enjoy jazz, transforms the city's waterfront into a stage for renowned jazz artists, creating an appealing ambiance under the summer sky.

3. Indie Sounds and New Artists

The music culture in Nova Scotia is not just rich in tradition, but it is also a center for current and indie performers. Cities such as Halifax are recognized for their dynamic live music venues, which provide platforms for budding artists to display their abilities. There's always the chance to discover the next great thing in the independent music scene, from quaint coffee shops to hip underground pubs.

4. Sound Symphony

For those who enjoy classical music, the Nova Scotia Symphony Orchestra puts on enthralling concerts that capture the beauty and majesty of the genre. The symphony delivers an audio experience that transcends time and location, with timeless compositions by renowned composers and unique collaborations.

5. Theatrical Wonders

Music and performance are harmoniously intertwined in Nova Scotia's theatrical presentations. The Neptune Theatre in Halifax is a creative hotspot, presenting everything from Broadway classics to contemporary pieces. The theater brings stories to life with each performance through a symphony of acting, music, and stagecraft.

6. Musical Getaways for Two

Away from the bustling cities, Nova Scotia's smaller towns and seaside villages provide the rare opportunity to enjoy live music in intimate settings. Local artists mesmerize audiences with sincere performances in small settings, typically tucked away from main roadways. These hidden jewels offer an escape from the mundane and an opportunity to engage profoundly with the music and the performers.

7. Sites of Musical Heritage

The rich history of Nova Scotia is commemorated not only via its music but also through the heritage places that have created its musical landscape. From the Celtic Music Interpretive Centre in Judique to the Black Cultural Centre for Nova Scotia in Dartmouth, these organizations preserve and promote the musical heritage of the province's diverse cultures.

Live music and performances are more than simply entertainment in Nova Scotia; they are a way of life that reflects the province's profound connection to its past as well as its embrace of the present. Whether you're thumping your toes to traditional jigs, swaying to indie songs, or being swept away by symphonic strings, Nova Scotia provides an exquisite symphony of sound that resonates in the hearts of everyone who encounter it.

CHAPTER 5: ACCOMMODATION AND TRANSPORTATION

Hotels and Resorts Exquisite Getaways

Nova Scotia, located in the heart of Canada's coastal beauty, offers a stunning combination of rocky coastline, historic monuments, and warm friendliness. Whether you're looking for a relaxing getaway or an action-packed vacation, the province has a wide choice of hotels and resorts to suit any traveler's needs.

1. The Algonquin Resort

The Algonquin Resort in St. Andrews by the Sea, Nova Scotia, is perched along the scenic Passamaquoddy Bay and is a testimony to elegance and history. This beautiful 19th-century resort flawlessly blends Victorian grandeur with modern conveniences. Guests can enjoy stunning ocean views, revitalizing spa treatments, and a round of golf at the famed Algonquin Golf Course.

2. White Point Beach Resort: Coastal peace

White Point Beach Resort is a true paradise for anyone looking for a coastal vacation. This family-owned resort on Nova Scotia's South Shore provides small cottages and accommodations with views of a gorgeous beach. Kayaking, guided treks, and nightly bonfires allow visitors to immerse themselves in the natural splendor of the area.

3. Secluded Luxury at Digby Pines Golf Resort and Spa

The Digby Pines Golf Resort & Spa, which overlooks the gorgeous Annapolis Basin, provides an excellent setting for relaxation. This Tudor-style resort features luxurious accommodations, a championship golf course, and a world-class spa. Enjoy fresh seafood meals while admiring the magnificent views of the water, or visit neighboring sites like the ancient town of Annapolis Royal.

4. Keltic Lodge Resort and Spa: The Charm of Cape Breton

The Keltic Lodge Resort and Spa offers a magnificent hideaway within the Cape Breton Highlands National Park. The resort, which overlooks the Gulf of St. Lawrence, provides attractive rooms as well as access to outdoor activities such as trekking along the Cabot Trail. Don't pass up the opportunity to sample local food at the Purple Thistle Dining Room, which features spectacular sunset views.

5. The Oak Island Resort & Conference Center

Maritime Mysteries

Oak Island Resort and Conference Centre is an appealing option for individuals who are interested in mysteries and marine tales. The resort, which is located on the famed Oak Island, offers an intriguing blend of history and modern comforts. Guests can partake in the island's fabled treasure search, relax in the spa, or participate in a variety of water activities along Mahone Bay.

6. Riverside Retreat at Liscombe Lodge Resort and Conference Centre

Liscombe Lodge Resort, tucked away in the bush along the Eastern Shore, offers a tranquil respite along the Liscombe River. The surrounding nature welcomes travelers to hike, fish, and kayak, while rustic cabins and lodge rooms provide pleasant accommodations. The lodge's welcoming atmosphere and closeness to Kejimkujik National Park make it a popular choice for nature lovers.

The hotels and resorts in Nova Scotia provide a rich tapestry of experiences, ranging from ancient elegance to rough coastal beauty. Whether you're looking for relaxation, adventure, or a little of both, these lodgings provide an ideal home base for exploring this Canadian province's breathtaking scenery and welcoming hospitality.

Bed & Breakfast
Beautiful Bed and Breakfasts in Picturesque Locations

The region has a variety of attractive bed and breakfasts (B&BS) that cater to both comfort and a genuine feeling of local culture for guests looking for an intimate and pleasant hotel experience. Let's take a deeper look at the enchanting world of Bed & Breakfasts in Nova Scotia, from historic mansions to beach retreats.

1. Historic Elegance and Contemporary Comfort

Bed & breakfasts in Nova Scotia frequently occupy beautifully restored historic homes, oozing old-world charm while providing modern facilities. Many of these B&BS are located in historic towns like Lunenburg, Annapolis Royal, and Wolf Ville, whose cobblestone streets and colonial buildings transport visitors back in time. Rooms with old furniture, beautiful woodwork, and comfortable fireplaces provide an atmosphere that reflects the region's rich past.

2. Beautiful Coastal Retreats

For those drawn to the enchantment of the Atlantic Ocean, Nova Scotia's coastal bed and breakfasts provide stunning vistas and easy access to the water's edge. Imagine waking up to the sound of waves breaking on the shore and sitting down to a fully prepared breakfast while staring out at the horizon. These B&BS provide an idyllic environment for relaxation and renewal, from the rocky cliffs of Peggy's Cove to the calm shores of Mahone Bay.

3. Culinary Delights and Local Flavors

The ability to sample the local flavors is one of the delights of visiting a Nova Scotia bed and breakfast. Many B&B owners take delight in serving farm-to-table breakfasts made with products purchased locally from orchards, farms, and fisheries. Guests can sample delectable meals such as freshly made blueberry scones, lobster eggs Benedict, and maple-infused delights that highlight the region's culinary heritage.

4. Personalized Experiential Learning

The intimate character of B&BS encourages a deep bond between guests and hosts. Innkeepers frequently go above and above to ensure that their visitors enjoy an unforgettable stay. Whether it's providing personalized advice for exploring the area, sharing stories about the region's history, or organizing unique activities like guided hikes or wine tours, these hosts create a welcoming environment that makes visitors feel like they're a part of the local community.

5. The Gateway to the Attractions of Nova Scotia

Many Nova Scotia bed and breakfasts are strategically positioned near some of the province's most recognizable attractions. From the spectacular scenic journey along the Cabot Trail to the historic Citadel Hill in Halifax, guests can utilize their B&B as a pleasant and convenient base for enjoying the region's many wonders.

Campgrounds and RV Parks

Nova Scotia's craggy coastline, gorgeous lakes, lush forests, and quaint towns make it a great location for camping and RV vacations. This province has something for every type of camper, whether you're looking for an isolated wilderness adventure or a family-friendly campground. Here's a look at some of Nova Scotia's best camping and RV parks:

1. National Park of the Cape Breton Highlands

This national park, located along the famous Cabot Trail, offers breathtaking coastal views, green slopes, and a choice of camping possibilities. Choose between front-country campgrounds with basic facilities and backcountry sites for a more rustic experience. The park offers hiking routes, wildlife sights, and cultural activities.

2. Kejimkujik National Park is located in northern Canada.

Kejimkujik, known for its rich Mi'kmaq history and unique ecosystems, provides both a mainland and backcountry camping experience. Paddle through pristine waterways, wander through ancient woodlands, and see petroglyphs that reveal indigenous history.

3. Provincial Park Blomidon

Blomidon Provincial Park, perched above towering sea cliffs overlooking the Bay of Fundy, is a refuge for beachcombers and hikers. The tides here are among the highest in the world, making for an unforgettable natural sight. Campsites are hidden within woodland areas, creating a tranquil setting for your camping vacation.

4. The Provincial Park of the Islands

This park covers many islands in Mahone Bay and is accessible by ferry. It's a kayaker's dream, with calm seas to explore and beautiful beaches to unwind on. The park provides modest amenities, ensuring a genuine island camping experience.

5. Provincial Park Ellenwood Lake

This park, located near Yarmouth, has a beautiful lake with a sandy beach, making it a popular site for swimming and picnicking. The park has both wooded and lakeside campsites, and the surrounding area is full of attractive fishing communities.

6. Provincial Park Dollar Lake

This park is ideal for families because it has a huge sandy beach, supervised swimming, and a variety of recreational activities. The campground has modern conveniences as well as easy access to hiking paths. The beautiful magnificence of the surrounding Musquodoboit Valley is well worth investigating.

7. Provincial Park Laurie

This park, located along the Northumberland Shore, is well-known for its warm waters and sandy beaches. Campsites are tucked in the woods, while Pictou, a nearby town, offers historical sites and local seafood eating.

8. Campground and Cottages at Hubbards Beach

Hubbards Beach is an excellent choice for anyone looking for a more laid-back coastal camping experience. The park has RV sites with seaside views, and Hubbards, a nearby community, is noted for its farmers' market and live music events.

9. Yogi Bear's Jelly stone Park is a theme park owned by Yogi Bear.

This campsite is ideal for families because it offers themed weekends, outdoor movie nights, and a variety of activities for youngsters. It's a fun-filled place for families visiting the Annapolis Valley, with RV sites and cottage rentals.

10. Cottages and Laurie's Motor Inn

This lodging offers RV sites, cottages, and motel rooms in the center of the Bras d'Or Lake region. Boating, fishing, and stunning sunsets over the lake are all available.

How to Get Around

Knowing the ins and outs of transportation alternatives is essential whether you're a local or a guest seeing this lovely province. Nova Scotia has a variety of options for exploring its beauties, from automobile rentals to public transit.

1. Car Rentals: The Open Road Freedom

Renting a car in Nova Scotia allows you to explore the province's different landscapes at your leisure. You'll have the freedom to go off the beaten road with several vehicle rental businesses available at major airports and cities including Halifax, Sydney, and Yarmouth. When contemplating an automobile rental, keep the following considerations in mind:

Booking in Advance: To guarantee the vehicle type you like during peak tourist seasons, book your car hire well in advance.

Driving Restrictions: Learn about Canadian driving restrictions, such as seatbelt usage, speed limits, and road signs.

Fueling: Gas stations are plentiful, particularly in urban locations. When visiting more rural areas of the province, be prepared for lengthier distances between stations.

Scenic Drives: Don't miss the Cabot Trail, which offers breathtaking vistas of the Gulf of St. Lawrence and the Atlantic Ocean.

2. Using Public Transportation to Get Around Cities

The bigger cities in Nova Scotia, such as Halifax and Sydney, have reliable and affordable public transportation networks. Here's what you should know:

Halifax Transit: Halifax's public transportation system consists of buses and boats. The ferry service not only provides a convenient mode of transportation but also provides spectacular views of the city's cityscape from the sea.

Cape Breton Transit: Cape Breton Transit operates buses in Sydney that connect various regions of the city, making it easier to see local sites without driving.

Fares and Passes: Halifax Transit and Cape Breton Transit both provide a variety of fare options, including single-ride fares and day passes, which can give significant discounts for frequent riders.

Schedules: To plan your trips more efficiently, familiarize yourself with the schedules and routes ahead of time.

3. Rural Adventures: Getting Out of the City

While public transit is more common in cities, seeing rural Nova Scotia may necessitate a little extra planning:

Shuttle Services: Some areas provide shuttle services to famous tourist locations such as national parks and historic sites.

Tour Packages: Consider taking guided tours that transport you to popular locations, removing the need to wander on your own.

Taxis and Ridesharing: In some places, ridesharing platforms and taxi services can let you travel short distances more conveniently.

The Top 5 Hotels in Nova Scotia for Luxurious Retreats

The province is home to several excellent hotels that provide exceptional service, breathtaking views, and unrivaled luxury. We showcase the top 5 hotels in Nova Scotia that promise an amazing visit in this post.

1. Autograph Collection, the Algonquin Resort St. Andrews by the Sea

This ancient hotel, located in the picturesque town of St. Andrews-by-the-Sea, is a jewel of elegance and grandeur. The Autograph Collection's Algonquin Resort mixes historical elegance with modern conveniences. Guests can enjoy panoramic views of Passamaquoddy Bay, spa treatments, gourmet dining, and a round of golf on the renowned course. The Algonquin is a unique place thanks to its traditional architecture and genuine welcome.

2. Digby Pines Golf and Spa Resort

Digby Pines, which overlooks the scenic Annapolis Basin, combines old-world elegance with modern conveniences. This iconic resort offers luxuriously designed rooms, a difficult golf course, and a relaxing spa. Guests can visit the nearby town of Digby, which is famous for its scallop fleet and bustling cultural scene. Digby Pines offers a traditional Nova Scotian experience, whether relaxing by the outdoor heated pool or dining on seasonal food.

3. Hotel Marriott Halifax Harbourfront

This Marriott hotel on the waterfront in the heart of Halifax offers stunning views of the harbor and convenient access to the city's attractions. The luxury rooms and suites offer a relaxing escape, while the on-site dining selections highlight regional tastes. This hotel is great for both business and leisure guests due to its proximity to prominent attractions such as the Maritime Museum of the Atlantic and the Halifax Seaport Farmers' Market.

4. Fox Harb'r Hotel

Fox Harb'r Resort is a true haven of tranquility for those looking for a private retreat. This premium resort provides a private golf course, a full-service spa, and upmarket accommodations ranging from small rooms to beautiful estate residences on a large estate overlooking Northumberland Strait. Outdoor activities such as horseback riding, clay shooting, and boating are available to guests, making it an ideal escape for nature lovers.

5. White Point Beach Hotel

White Point Beach Resort, perched along a gorgeous length of shoreline, is a family-friendly place that embodies the essence of Nova Scotia's natural beauty. The resort provides a relaxed ambiance and spectacular ocean views with its comfortable cottages and pleasant lodge accommodations. Guests can explore the beach, participate in organized activities, or simply relax in front of the fireplace. The resort's commitment to sustainability and community involvement adds to its allure.

Safety Recommendations

However, just as in any other situation, it is critical to emphasize safety to maintain a good and secure environment for all. Here are some important safety considerations to keep in mind while visiting Nova Scotia, whether you're touring the lovely coastal towns, trekking through lush forests, or enjoying the local cuisine:

1. Ocean Security

The coastline of Nova Scotia is beautiful, but the tides and currents can be dangerous. Check tidal schedules before going to the beach, and use caution when swimming, kayaking, or boating.

If you're not an experienced swimmer, stick to shallow waters. Keep a watch on children near the water at all times, and never turn your back on the ocean.

2. Wildlife Conservation

Moose, black bears, and coyotes are among the natural species found in Nova Scotia. Keep a safe distance and avoid feeding wild animals when exploring outdoors. This avoids potentially hazardous contacts.

When hiking or camping, keep your food safe to avoid attracting animals to your campsite.

3. Driving Security

Follow speed limits and traffic signs when driving along the Cabot Trail or through Halifax. In some regions, roads might be winding and narrow, necessitating particular caution.

Be ready for drastically changing weather conditions, particularly in the winter. Keep a winter survival kit in your car, which should include warm clothing, blankets, and emergency supplies.

4. Outdoor Activities

The landscapes of Nova Scotia provide amazing chances for hiking, biking, and exploration. Inform someone of your plans and expected return time before departing on any expedition.

Wear activity-appropriate attire and footwear. Check the weather forecast before venturing out, and always bring a map, compass, or GPS device with you.

5. Activities on the Water

If you're going boating, kayaking, or fishing, be sure you have all of the appropriate safety gear, such as life jackets and communication devices.

To guarantee a safe and pleasurable day on the water, become familiar with local boating regulations and navigational signs.

6. Emergency Planning

Save vital phone numbers on your phone, such as local emergency services and your country's embassy or consulate.

Consider obtaining travel insurance if you are not a resident to cover medical emergencies and unforeseen trip modifications.

7. Cultural Awareness

Nova Scotia, including Indigenous settlements, has a rich history and culture. Respect the local norms and traditions, as well as the region you're exploring. Before approaching private property or Indigenous territory, obtain permission.

8. Public Health Recommendations

Keep up to current on local COVID-19 standards and limits in light of ongoing global health issues. To protect yourself and others, follow mask mandates, social distance guidelines, and other recommendations.

By following these safety precautions, you may make the most of your time in Nova Scotia while also insuring your own and others' safety. Remember that careful and educated behavior makes everyone's experience safer and more enjoyable.

Emergency Phone Numbers

The picturesque province of Nova Scotia, tucked along Canada's eastern coast, places a premium on the safety and well-being of its citizens and visitors. Being prepared for emergencies is vital, and having the correct contacts on hand can make all the difference in life-threatening situations. Whether you're a local or a visitor to this marine wonder, knowing who to contact in an emergency can bring a sense of security and peace of mind.

911 is the number to dial for emergency services.

Dialing 911 in the event of an emergency danger, injury, or life-threatening scenario is the quickest and most effective approach to seeking assistance. This emergency hotline connects you to police, fire, medical, and other important resources that can respond quickly to your needs. 911 should be your first contact in the event of a medical emergency, a fire, a crime, or any other issue requiring immediate care.

To report a power outage in Nova Scotia, call 1-877-428-6004.

Power outages can occur for a variety of reasons, such as weather occurrences or technical faults. If you have a power outage, reporting it to Nova Scotia Power can assist them in identifying and resolving the problem as soon as possible. Having this number on hand is especially essential during storms or other severe weather when power outages are more frequent.

811 for Non-Emergency Medical Advice

Health Link 811 is an excellent resource for non-emergency medical issues. You can reach registered nurses by dialing 811, who can provide medical advice, information on symptoms, and guidance on where to obtain appropriate medical care. This service is especially useful if you are unsure about the seriousness of a health problem and require expert assistance without going to the emergency department.

1-800-565-8161 (Poison Control Center).

Poisoning by accident can happen to anyone, especially children and pets. If you suspect someone has swallowed a dangerous chemical, contact the Poison Control Centre right once. This helpline can provide advice on how to handle the problem while waiting for professional medical assistance.

Municipal Police Departments

It is also critical to know the non-emergency contact numbers for your local police stations. While 911 should be used in an emergency, these numbers can be used to report non-emergencies or to obtain general information:

Halifax Regional Police Department: (902) 490-5020

(902) 563-5151 - Cape Breton Regional Police

RCMP (Royal Canadian Mounted Police): There are various detachments in Nova Scotia.

Community Resources and Assistance Services

Aside from emergency hotlines, knowing about local community resources and support programs can be extremely valuable. Shelters, crisis lines, mental health services, and organizations dedicated to supporting vulnerable populations during emergencies are examples of such resources.

Remember that planning is essential for dealing with emergencies efficiently. Familiarize yourself with the numerous emergency contacts, develop a communication plan with your family and loved ones, and remain up to date on local emergency protocols. By taking these precautions, you help to ensure the safety and resilience of Nova Scotia's communities.

Health and Medical Services

1. Infrastructure for Healthcare

Nova Scotia's healthcare infrastructure includes a network of hospitals, clinics, and medical centers that serve the province's diversified healthcare needs. There are several tertiary care institutions in the province, including the QEII Health Sciences Centre in Halifax, which offers specialized medical services, cutting-edge therapies, and complex surgical procedures. Furthermore, community hospitals and health clinics are located across the province, ensuring that both urban and rural residents have access to healthcare services.

2. Skilled Healthcare Personnel

The province is proud of its highly skilled and dedicated healthcare workers. Nova Scotia's medical personnel is well-trained and dedicated to providing the best possible treatment, from doctors and nurses to specialists and allied health workers. To address potential manpower shortfalls, the province actively recruits healthcare professionals from within Canada and internationally.

3. E-Health and Telemedicine

The province of Nova Scotia has embraced technological advances in healthcare delivery. Telemedicine services allow patients to receive medical consultations at a distance, which is especially useful for individuals who live in rural or remote places. E-health initiatives have resulted in electronic medical records, which improve patient care coordination and reduce test and treatment duplication.

4. Wellness and Mental Health

Recognizing the significance of mental health, Nova Scotia has taken steps to improve access to mental health services. To address diverse mental health concerns, the province provides crisis intervention services, psychotherapy, and community-based programs. To ensure a holistic approach to well-being, mental health is integrated into primary care settings.

5. Health Promotion and Prevention

Preventive care is an essential component of Nova Scotia's healthcare plan. Public health programs and initiatives emphasize healthy lifestyle choices such as regular exercise, balanced nutrition, and smoking cessation. Vaccinations are also promoted by the province to reduce the spread of communicable diseases.

6. Research and Development

The healthcare system in Nova Scotia is not only concerned with delivering care but also with developing medical knowledge. Innovative therapies, medical technologies, and healthcare delivery techniques are being investigated by research institutions in collaboration with healthcare facilities. This dedication to research aids in the continuing improvement of healthcare methods.

7. Initiatives for Indigenous Health

The province recognizes Indigenous populations' distinct healthcare needs. Collaboration between healthcare providers and Indigenous leaders aims to reduce health inequities and provide Indigenous populations with culturally sensitive care.

Basic Phrases

Whether you're a traveler eager to explore Nova Scotia or a resident looking to connect with the local culture, learning basic phrases in both French and Mi'kmaq can enhance your experience and foster meaningful interactions.

Basic French Phrases

1. Bonjour (bohn-zhoor) - Hello

2. S'il vous plaît (seel voo pleh) - Please

3. Merci (mehr-see) - Thank you

4. Excusez-moi (ehk-skew-zay mwah) - Excuse me

5. Oui (wee)- Yes

6. Non (noh) - No

7. Parlez-vous anglais? (Par-lei voo ahn-glay?) - Do you speak English?

8. Combien ça coûte? (kohm-byen sah koot ?) - How much does it cost?

9. L'addition, s'il vous plaît (la-dee-syon, seel voo pleh) - The check, please

10. Où est... ? (oo eh... ?) - Where is...?

Basic Mi'kmaq Phrases:

1. Kwe' (kway)- Hello

2. Pijilita'suti (pee-jee-lee-tah-soo-dee) - Please

3. M'sit No'kmaq (m-sit noh-guh-mah) - Thank you

4. Ula'si (oo-lah-see) - Excuse me

5. E' (ay) - Yes

6. Aji (ah-jee) - No

7. Akwiten (ah-kwih-ten) - Do you speak English?

8. Pjila'si mawlmawl (pee-jee-lah-see mawl-mawl) - How much does it cost?

9. Kisiku'l (kee-see-kool) - The check/bill

10. Ta'n tel-kisi (tahn tayl-kee-see) - Where is...?

Learning these basic phrases in both French and Mi'kmaq can greatly enhance your experience while exploring Nova Scotia. The Acadian influence is palpable in the province, especially in regions like the Annapolis Valley and the Chéticamp area, where French heritage is celebrated through local events, cuisine, and traditions.

Additionally, engaging with the Mi'kmaq language showcases your respect for the indigenous culture of Nova Scotia. The Mi'kmaq people have a deep connection to the land and the waters, and their language reflects their spiritual bond with nature.

BONUS: CURATED SEASONAL EVENT CALENDAR

Here is a seasonally selected event schedule to help you plan your vacation and make the most of your time in Nova Scotia.

Spring: May apple Blossom Festival: The Annapolis Valley celebrates the coming of spring with a week-long event that includes parades, live music, fireworks, and, of course, the magnificent sight of apple blossoms in full bloom.

Tulip event (May-June): During this event, Halifax's Public Gardens are transformed into a sea of bright tulips, providing an ideal backdrop for strolls and vibrant photo opportunities.

Craft beer fans may enjoy tastings, brewery tours, and special events across the province during Nova Scotia Craft Beer Week (May), which highlights the region's thriving craft beer culture.

Summer: Lobster Festivals (June-July): Indulge in Nova Scotia's most iconic seafood at one of the region's lobster festivals, complete with lobster suppers, live music, and maritime entertainment.

The Halifax International Busker Festival (July-August) brings street performers, acrobats, comedians, and musicians from all over the world to the waterfront, creating a lively and exciting scene.

Nova Scotia Multicultural Festival (August): Celebrate cultures from around the world with food, music, dance, and art, presenting a diverse tapestry of experiences.

Fall: Halifax Pop Explosion (October): Music fans flock to this multi-venue music festival, which features a wide roster of local and international acts and highlights the city's thriving music culture.

Annapolis Valley Apple Harvest Festival (September-October): Celebrate the bounty of the harvest season in the gorgeous Annapolis Valley with apple picking, corn mazes, wagon rides, and other family-friendly activities.

Celtic Colors International Festival (October): Immerse yourself in the heart of Cape Breton's Celtic culture with concerts, workshops, and community events that feature traditional music and dance.

Halifax Christmas Market (November to December): Get into the holiday season with a European-inspired Christmas market in downtown Halifax, which offers artisanal products, festive food, and a comfortable ambiance.

Winter Ice wine Festival (February): Enjoy cold-climate wines from Nova Scotia, including exquisite ice-wines, at this festival that blends wine tastings with seasonal activities.

Winter Surfing Championships in Nova Scotia (January-February): See adventurous surfers take on the icy Atlantic waves, demonstrating their talents and passion for the water even in the cold months.

This seasonal event calendar only scratches the surface of what's going on in Nova Scotia throughout the year. There is an event for every sort of tourist, whether you are drawn to natural beauty, cultural diversity, or culinary delights.

Nova Scotia Travel Journal

Date: Transport:

Weather

Checklist For This Trip	Places:

Notes

Nova Scotia Travel Journal

Date: _____   Transport: _____

Weather: ☁️ ☀️ 💧 🌙 ❄️

Checklist For This Trip	Places:

Notes

105 | Nova Scotia Travel Guide

Nova Scotia Travel Journal

Date:　　　　　　　　Transport:

Weather

Checklist For This Trip

Places:

Notes

Nova Scotia Travel Journal

Date: _____   Transport: _____

Weather

Checklist For This Trip

Places:

Notes

Nova Scotia Travel Journal

Date: _____ Transport: _____

Weather

Checklist For This Trip

Places:

Notes

Nova Scotia Travel Journal

Date: _____ Transport: _____

Weather: ☁ ☀ 💧 🌙 ❄

Checklist For This Trip	Places:
	Notes

Nova Scotia Travel Journal

Date: _____ Transport: _____

Weather: ☁ ☀ 💧 🌙 ❄

Checklist For This Trip

Places:

Notes

Nova Scotia Travel Journal

Date: _____ Transport: _____

Weather

Checklist For This Trip

Places:

Notes

111 | Nova Scotia Travel Guide

Nova Scotia Travel Journal

Date: Transport:

Weather

Checklist For This Trip

Places:

Notes